GOD AT WORK
Through the Voices of Children

Text © 2000 by
Saint Meinrad Archabbey

Published by One Caring Place
Abbey Press
St. Meinrad, Indiana 47577

All rights reserved.
No part of this book may be used or
reproduced in any manner without
written permission of the publisher,
except in the case of brief
quotations embodied in critical
articles and reviews.

Library of Congress Catalog Number
00-101212

ISBN 0-87029-341-9

Printed in the United States of America

GOD AT WORK Through the Voices of Children

Edited by R. Philip Etienne

ONE CARING PLACE

Abbey Press
St. Meinrad, Indiana 47577

To Sophie and Kyle—

Through you and because of you,
I know that God loves us.
I see that love every day
in your eyes.

Introduction

As a parent of two small children, I have taken great interest in this book from its inception. Not only can I relate with the many situations illustrated in the following pages, but, like the many authors who have contributed, I have often found that children are the great equalizers in life. No matter how bad things seem at times, a simple smile or an "I love you, Dad" from my kids can make everything else so insignificant.

The wonderful thing about children is: no matter how unruly or naïve they may seem at times, they are basically honest and know how to cut straight to the heart of matters. With them, there are few gray areas. They don't want excuses and weighted responses ... they expect the truth and know when they don't hear it.

Children are not saints by any means—at least not mine. They fight with each other. They tend to overlook their precious honesty trait when I'm trying to find out who broke the lamp. They sometimes even question my wisdom—heaven forbid! But what makes them so amazing, and so inspires me, is the fact that they always end up playing by the rules: children seem physically, emotionally, and spiritually unable to carry for long the weight of an untruth told or a misdeed done.

Now, a cynic may argue that children just haven't yet learned how to be properly deceitful ... that they'll acquire that "talent" with more life experiences. But I'd rather cherish their purity and innocence. I'd rather strive to regain those open and forgiving qualities in myself. And if that makes me appear child-like, well ... so much the better.

—R. Philip Etienne

No one has yet fully realized the wealth of sympathy, kindness and generosity hidden in the soul of a child.
— Emma Goldman

The Gift of the Kingdom
By Kass Perry-Dotterweich

During the final week of Advent, I often noticed my five-year-old son, Joseph, strolling through the house in what looked like a daze. Now Joseph always has marched to the beat of a drum the rest of us don't hear, but this behavior seemed especially peculiar to me.

"What are you doing, Joseph?" I asked one afternoon after watching this routine for several days in a row. "Oh, nothing," Joseph responded with a slight smile that suggested something playfully mysterious. "Well," I thought to myself, "whatever it is, he isn't doing any harm to himself or anyone else—and he seems to be having a good time." As a working mother with six children—in the final days before Christmas—I just had too many other things to do to probe further.

Christmas morning dawned with a frenzy of excitement and chaos. Then, as the gift-giving got underway, I thought it was peculiar when Joseph pulled out from under the tree *seven presents*—one for his father, one for me, and one for each of his siblings. The presents, ranging from small jewelry-sized boxes to shoe boxes, perplexed me further. Joseph was not a "craft" person; he never would have *made* presents for everyone. And I *knew* Joseph did not have money to *buy* presents.

As I started to unwrap my present from Joseph, I watched the rest of the family open theirs. And I watched the delight explode! Jerome pulled out his Little League spikes; he had borrowed a pair all summer because he couldn't find his own. Christine unwrapped her hair brush, missing for weeks. I discovered a small porcelain Madonna and Child statue that always sat on my desk, usually buried under bills and correspondence.

And so it went. Everyone unwrapped a "present" that was *already theirs,* things Joseph had either found or knew that we simply did not know we already owned. He gave each of us our own treasures, and no one was disappointed. In the laughter and surprise of those moments, I realized that Joseph knew the secret of the true meaning of Christmas, of "peace on earth." Blessed are you who give to others that which is already theirs, for yours is the kingdom of God.

If I had my life to live over I would have sat on the lawn with my children and not worried about grass stains.

—Erma Bombeck

Missing Mommy
By Jean Ubelhor

The day started out as many others before. I was always in a rush, always trying to accomplish too much in a day's time, not giving my full attention to anything or anyone. It seemed as though the kids were always underfoot, but I guess that's where four-year-olds and 18-month-olds are supposed to be.

Many times I had heard that these were the best days, that the kids would grow up too soon. I couldn't see it though. I was blinded by the overflowing work on my desk, the pile of bills in the mail and the long list of things to do.

By the time the kids woke up that morning, I was already on

edge, and the turtle-pace at which the kids were moving only aggravated me more. "Why can't you move any faster?" I snapped at my four-year-old as she tried to get dressed. In the kitchen, her younger brother dumped cereal on the floor and crushed it with his feet.

I was trying to hurry them along for a trip to the local store. As part of a Girl Scout project, a girl from our parish had placed a box at church to collect coloring books and puzzles for kids in the local hospitals—so we were going to purchase a few items to donate.

I knew I would have to make it clear that we were picking out items to give away, not to keep. I explained to my daughter that the kids at the hospital needed things to do because they were sick and missed their mommies and daddies when they couldn't be with them. She nodded as if she understood.

I pulled into the church parking lot and quickly shuttled the kids inside. As we loaded our goodies into the container, I again mentioned that the things we bought would help the kids feel better. "I hope so," my daughter said, "It's sad to miss Mommy."

I assumed she meant she missed me during the times she was at Grandma's house or when I had a meeting to attend. But she gave me an answer that was much more clear: "I miss my Mommy when you get mad at me and don't smile," she said.

Children are the hands by which we take hold of heaven.

— Henry Ward Beecher

Mercy Me

By Tom McGrath

I let my daughter fall from a swing one day. She was an adventurous two-year-old who wanted to swing on the "big-kid fwings," as she called them. I let her.

At first, I watched her closely; but as the drone of pushing and pushing her on that swing wore on, my attention drifted. Just once, I pushed a little too low and a little too hard and she flipped over and fell on the asphalt right smack on her head.

I was devastated. How could a father allow such a thing to happen? I imagined all the dutiful parents on the playground looking at me in scorn. My daughter cried, shocked that her daddy could let her down so.

I scooped her up and held her, I rubbed her head and kissed it. I murmured apologies and soothing words. Inside, I berated myself, wondering what kind of a father could let this happen. I felt unworthy.

At that moment, my daughter consoled me. Her eyes were still wet, but she smiled. She looked at me, and I asked if she was better.

"Fwing better," she said, smiling and trying to boost herself up on the swing once again. I had not been the perfect dad. Though the lapse was a brief and minor one, it stood for all the mistakes I knew I was sure to make down the line. And yet, because in previous days in her young life she had known mercy, my daughter was able to shower mercy back on me as well. God worked through her in that instant, and I knew it.

We do not have to go far to catch echoes of (God's) mysterious, cosmic dance. When we see children in a moment when they are really children ... the awakening, the turning inside out of all values, the 'newness' .... and the purity of vision that makes themselves evident, provide a glimpse of the cosmic dance.

— Thomas Merton

Our Children: Directors of Our Soul

By Kathy Coffey

The search is on for a spiritual director, but a good one is hard to find. For once, parents may be fortunate. In the quest for spiritual direction, we need look no further than our own children.

Experienced parents may think this proposal either idealistic or facetious. What stretch of the imagination could find a guru in the toddler smearing strawberry yogurt on the rug or in the teenager who drags reluctant parents on the roller-coaster ride of changing hormones? How could we look to kids for spiritual help when they often cause our crises?

Such reactions are realistic; they were mine when I discovered this idea in James Finley's book, *Merton's Palace of Nowhere*. He says, "Our real spiritual directors, our real gurus, are our loved ones who place upon us unexplainable burdens, force us to proceed out from our narcissistic prison into a selfless encounter in love."

Our children do invite us to countless places where we'd rather not be—often at 3:00 a.m. Yet, their very insistence prevents us from wallowing in a puddle of apathy. How can we disappoint their need for tradition, their longing for transcendence, their right to rooted security?

In an ironic twist, our efforts to give them these values gift us in return. As we try to parent well, we become people of larger vision; we become less conscious of meeting our own needs and turn toward nurturing others.

That, however, is not the only gift. Finley explains further that the spiritual master is one in whom God finds no obstacle. In that case, our children can be masters: unselfconscious oases of beauty and grace. Most of them have not yet learned to hide behind adult cosmetics, to camouflage their natural responses with artificial masks. In them, the divine light shines.

By the same token, they are totally present to now. No one needs to convince them of what Plato called "the indescribable marvel of reality." When they dance, every toe crinkles, each plump arm circles wide. They have no preoccupations; they don't glance nervously at watches. They embody the advice of Anthony DeMello: "The most important thing in the world is whatever we happen to be doing at the moment."

If our divided selves are keeping a frantic pace, we may miss the gracious givenness of now. A slow learner, I worried distractedly through three children before I learned to appreciate my youngest daughter. Now, her slightest gesture nudges me toward God.

I watch, for instance, as she welcomes a pancake. I might shovel it in, keeping one eye on the clock and one ear cocked for the honk of the carpool. She drizzles syrup over that golden brown circle in an artistic pattern and then savors each warm bite. Her breakfast shows me how contemplation means presence to what's real.

In the contemplative tradition, life is full of "tea ceremonies," the opportunities to pause and appreciate beauty we often take for granted. On occasion my daughter invites me to a tea party she has concocted. Ritually, we sip invisible beverages from doll-sized cups of white china painted in blue designs. She handles her cup with such care that I wonder why I often warn her not to spill milk or drop plates. In my constant, headlong rush, I am the one more likely to break the china than this small but considerate hostess. Reverence seems her birthright.

Furthermore, the master reassures the seeker that the path ends well without disappointment. In this role, our children lay clues like bread crumbs, as though the birds had not eaten Hansel and Gretel's trail and all the subtle hints point "home." In our pseudosophistication, we tend to miss the obvious. Our children act as lighthouses, seeing as Meister Eckhart did that "every caterpillar is full of God."

The presence of the master leaves no doubt of God's existence. I remember an atheist friend standing in the hospital nursery, admiring her newborn son. Blond and beautiful, he was curled contentedly in his bassinet, every toe perfect, every neuron intricately patterned, every cell healthy. Bundled in a flannel receiving blanket, he was pure gift. At that moment, his mother came closer to belief in a personal Creator than ever before in her life.

If we allow it, our children teach us a profound theology. The signature of a Creator marks every gesture, each low chuckle. Their trust in the Father and Mother God transfers to us. They assume we can make all things right. Nestling in our arms, they find a fortress from the world's craziness. Oddly enough, we rise to that expectation. We provide the safe harbor.

As we fill the plastic lunch boxes, we know they represent more than the simple nutrition of peanut butter and jelly. It is a sacramental food, this sandwich wrapped in cellophane. Having it, they have all they need to face a world which can be harsh and unnecessarily cruel.

But healthy children aren't much interested in negatives. Instead, they are consumed by curiosity: What floats? What burns? What sound does this instrument make? Where does that animal live? What makes people tick?

And we, who have never understood the rotation of the planets, find ourselves exploring it again. Making a silly ball orbit a red balloon, we point out excitedly: "This is the moon! This is the sun! And here—this sugar bowl is the earth!"

They invite us to some cosmic dance, and it doesn't matter to them if we haven't mastered the steps. In *New Seeds of Contemplation*, Thomas Merton writes: "We do not have to go far to catch echoes of (God's) mysterious, cosmic dance. When we see children in a moment when they are really children ... the awakening, the turning inside out of all values, the 'newness' ... and the purity of vision that makes themselves evident, provide a glimpse of the cosmic dance."

In *Taking Flight*, De Mello tells the story of a girl who did a beautiful job mowing the lawn. However, she left one shaggy, unmowed patch. Her father threatened not to pay her if the job was incomplete, but she refused to cut that grass. Investigating, he discovered a toad living in the center of the clump his daughter had so carefully preserved.

Through such experiences, our children teach us that love is untidy. As we clean up their spilled grape juice and gluey art projects, we can remind ourselves that perfect order would make the world a graveyard.

Their priorities are rightly ordered. What we see as so important—our careers, our images, our wardrobes—are pretty unimportant to them. They do not value our bank accounts, but our time. They dismiss our appearances; they call our truest selves. No substitutes will do when they so innocently invite us to the perplexing, dazzling world of committed love.

Finley concludes: "It is the love of ... And it is my love for ... my child that enables me to show God to him or her in himself or herself. Love is the epiphany of God in our poverty."

God's first epiphany came as a child, so it is not surprising that God should choose this way to come to us again. Through a child, God surprises us, confounds our silly notions, reveals us to ourselves, and guides us to God. So much guru in such a small person.

We find delight in the beauty and happiness of children that makes the heart too big for the body.
— Ralph Waldo Emerson

Bathtime Bulletin
By Lorri Malone

New parents do not sleep.

They exist in varying levels of unconsciousness, regardless of the time of day or the circumstances surrounding them. It's nearly impossible for them to surrender to the wiles of the sofa, bed, recliner or passenger seat for fear of two things: something will happen to their new, defenseless little infant; or someone will catch them unguarded and unjustly criticize their parenting skills.

Well, at least that's why I didn't sleep. New parents in general (new moms in particular) feel like they're on display for the world to judge them. Droves of people come to the house to see the new baby and in the process, decide if these novices have what it takes to cut the mustard as moms and dads. Even when my newborn son napped, I just couldn't allow my exhausted body and mind to relax. I did laundry, washed dishes, showered, swept cobwebs from high-reaching corners, folded towels … did anything to stay on top of the housework.

Not only did I not want to be caught with a dirty house, but a less-than-immaculate baby would surely signal negligence on my part. I was convinced that, along with good nutrition and proper rest, the only way to keep this child healthy was to quarantine him, away from other disease-bearing children, and to keep him clean. Suction that nose. Wash those tiny hands. Slide a wet wipe across that bottom. Pat those burps with a soft cloth. Keep him clean and his home clean and he'll stay healthy. It was an exhausting, never-ending cycle.

There was one particular Friday that had me in a panic. Company was coming and had given us short notice. Sleep deprivation had induced an almost manic paranoia in me. I was convinced that my dear old friends were on their way to size up my housekeeping habits, parenting skills, and postpartum appearance. I bustled to scrub the house, roll my hair, dip the child in a quick bath and dress him in his best baby attire.

I was busy working the shampoo into his scalp when he looked up at me and smiled the most precious smile I had ever seen. My heart melted. In that moment, I had an epiphany of sorts. "What am I doing?" I thought to myself. "God is trying to tell me something here. Who cares if this house is not decorator magazine perfect? This beautiful, healthy, *perfect* little angel-on-earth has just looked me in the eye and … eeewww."

Well, to put it delicately, he sent a "bulletin" that is more suitable for a diaper than the bath.

But right there in the tub it was indeed. At first, I was horrified. But my son just kept on smiling and soon I was smiling too. Crude as it first seemed, here at baby's bath time was God's way of telling me to slow it down, enjoy time with my baby, feel confident in my parenting skills. *And get some sleep.*

The soul is healed by being with children.

— Fyodor Dostoevsky

Through the Shadows
By Jeff Marks

Perhaps it was the autumn, but Margaret didn't know for sure. Not being a pensive person by nature, she couldn't figure out why today, a beautiful day in her favorite season, the thoughts flooded over her like the rapids of a river. Even during the past seven years of sickness, sadness, and struggle, Margaret never really allowed herself to be weighted down by oppressive thoughts—the doctors had told her there wasn't time for that; enjoy the rest of your life as much as you can; fight to stay up. And Margaret had done just that. But today was different: today she couldn't muster the energy or enthusiasm to forget her pain, to forget her looming death. Perhaps it was the autumn that made her this way, but Margaret allowed the thoughts to take control of her, to possess her so that there seemed to be very little of her left; only the dark thoughts of the reality of life.

No, it's not the autumn, Margaret thought, it's truly the end. Even all those years ago, when the doctors told her, "a year, maybe a year-and-a-half," she didn't believe it was the end. As the time rolled on, even when it seemed to everyone else, especially those doctors, that it was the end, Margaret never felt it to be so. She knew now, perhaps for the first time, that that was the reason for her thoughts this day: this was it, it was all over. The body tells you when to quit, and Margaret was quitting. It was time.

Just then, a rap at her bedroom window shook Margaret out of her thoughts. She looked out to see her little son, Kyle—his hands shading his big brown eyes so that they could see into her room. A smile came over Margaret's lips as she regarded her youngest child. His face was filthy, and dried leaves were tangled into his hair that always seemed to be one giant cow-lick anyway. His nose was running, but he took care of that with one swipe of his sweatshirt sleeve. "Mommy!" he shouted with great excitement, "I've made the biggest pile of leaves ever!"

Margaret laughed and looked into Kyle's eyes. She often thought that all those romance writers who gave the heroes blue eyes had missed the boat—they had obviously never looked into the eyes that she regarded now. Kyle's eyes were wondrous, beautiful, innocent. Even if he was bravely trying to hide something, his eyes never lied; they always gave him away. He rarely cried, but those eyes would mist over in an instant whenever sadness or the confusion of the grownup world came upon him. When happiness was anywhere near, those eyes could detect it, and people who knew Kyle were mesmerized by this detection. Margaret thought about how these eyes would be a liability for Kyle as he grew up. How could he be cunning and deceitful and get ahead in this rough world if those eyes always told the truth?

This thought caused her to sink back in darkness. Margaret wouldn't know how those eyes would look on an adult—she wouldn't be there to see it. The pain and darkness intensified as she thought about what those eyes would look like when Sam would break the news to him. What would those eyes register at her funeral?

Once again, Margaret was jolted out of her thoughts by the insistent pounding of small fists on her window. "Mommy, why don't you come see my leaf pile? I got a lawn chair out of the garage, so you can just sit there and you don't have to jump in them—you can watch me!"

"Sunshine, Mommy is very tired right now. I just can't. You go play." She looked closely at the eyes against her window and noticed they had developed that sheen—no tears, but the moist look of a young deer. Bambi's eyes, she thought, tenderly.

"Mommy, please come out." Margaret's heart felt as if it would burst within her. Not since Jesus Christ had said those words to Lazarus could they have been uttered with such power. Margaret realized, right then and there, that even though death was all around her, life was too—there just could not be one without the other. It's true, there was intense darkness in her life right now, but the light was there as well. "Walk not in the shadows": a line from a poem came to her suddenly. Yes, darkness and death were a part of life, a part even to be embraced, Margaret thought.

But just as Lazarus could not stay in the darkness of the tomb, she knew that she, too, had to reach for the light. And that light was personified right now in the eyes of a seven-year-old child. Walk not in the shadows.

As Margaret got up slowly to go outside to join her boy, she realized that indeed the real test was not walking in the shadows, or avoiding them completely, but walking through them. For it was only through their darkness, through their pain, that the light became a reality, a part of you. What an insight, Margaret thought to herself; what an insight to be gleaned from the eyes of a child. These were now her thoughts as she walked out the back door to go play in the leaves with her son.

I must take issue with the term "a mere child," for it has been my invariable experience that the company of a mere child is infinitely preferable to that of a mere adult.

—Fran Lebowitz

Out of the Mouths of Babes

By Rita Beer

When I was young, most children were taught to respect their parents and weigh their words ... you know, think before you speak. I started teaching my own children this wise practice as soon as I thought they were old enough to understand it.

However, there are those rare occasions when saying what's on one's mind is a good thing. And sometimes, your first reaction to a situation is the most honest one.

My daughter, Mindi, was always strong-willed and intelligent. As a child, she regularly spoke her mind and apologized later—if you know what I mean. She was brutally honest, but never tried to be unkind.

To put it simply, this little person was passionate about everything. If she was happy, she was extremely happy. If she was sad, the tears flowed freely. If she was angry ... look out! She loved deeply and forgave completely. She expected others to be honest and good because ... well, just because they should be.

One day, I was laboring in the kitchen over some unimportant craft project, when Mindi came bouncing into the room. She found me complaining half under my breath, yet loud enough for her to catch a few words.

She asked me what the problem was and I continued to complain. I listed people I knew who were so talented. At least they were good at something—even if it was just one thing. I grumbled about not being really great at anything. Her reply was, "But Mom, you're mediocre at *so many things.*"

I know the look on my face at that moment must have been priceless. I wasn't sure whether to be indignant or to weep at the most precious compliment I've ever received. Unlike some people who do only one thing well, in her eyes, I could do *everything*. I might not be the best, but giving the job my best effort was, in her opinion, admirable and good enough for her.

Grown men can learn from very little children for the hearts of little children are pure. Therefore, the Great Spirit may show to them many things which older people miss.

— Black Elk

A Child Can Teach Us
By Carol Troesch

We gathered to wait, awkwardly turning the pages of out-of-date magazines while we sat uncomfortably close and listened to the drone of the television. It was like being in an elevator with ugly chairs—social rules dictated that it would be unusual to start a conversation, or even look at another person. And it would be completely unheard of to grab the remote control and change channels to a program we'd probably all enjoy more.

The coffee pot in the corner beckoned us to grab a cup and relax, enjoy! My daughter, Emily, was occupied in the center of the floor, playing at a table full of blocks, oblivious to the long, torturous, drawn-out minutes.

Our vehicles were lined up in the parking lot. Pick-ups, mini-vans, compacts. One by one, they were brought in to be tinkered with, fixed, and winterized.

It was a great time of year for a car service department—the first breath of cold air indicated winter was on its way and the deer and sometimes icy roads led to many a fender-bender.

People were scattered decidedly around the small waiting room. No one was purposely sitting next to another; no one touched the remote.

A middle-aged man sat in the dead-center of the couch, daring anyone to sit beside him. He wore a hat advertising one of the latest truck models. New owner, I thought. I wondered why he was there: an accident, a routine check, or had he acquired a lemon?

Of course, I wasn't about to ask. Nothing about him was exactly inviting conversation.

A lady walked in and, like the rest of us, looked around—not at the room full of bored patrons, but at the worn, curled covers of magazines—in hopes of finding one that would occupy her for the long wait. I noticed that she was wearing two different shoes, and suddenly I wished I had someone with whom to share a silent grin.

Emily, at the tender age of 21 months, did not yet appreciate such moments. She was at the stage where wearing two different socks was absolutely routine.

In the midst of chuckling to myself, I was shocked to hear a break in the great silence—not by a mechanic with a question or a dreaded "It's worse than we thought" intro. It was Emily!

Apparently, she had decided that all of this silence was nonsense. She had told the lady with two different shoes "Hi!" and was now trying to trade magazines with her. I looked at the lady to be sure she was enjoying Emily's social graces, and, sure enough, she was.

When the lady reached down to tie one of her shoes, I heard her exclaim to herself, "Oh my." It was Emily who reminded her of the really important task at hand. "Shoes!" she said, "tie it!" And with that, she offered her own shoe in an attempt to share the moment.

Suddenly caught up in the excitement of newfound friends, Emily raced over to the couch, and—you guessed it—attempted to crawl right up beside the man on the couch. He didn't move or look away. He simply reached out to help her up.

She pointed out, in her own way, that she had noticed his cap. "Hat. Grandpa," she mused. The entire room shared in her innocent joy. When our mechanic finally walked in and handed over the bill, I wasn't sure I was ready to leave!

Never before had I seen the waiting room alive with such chatter and laughter. Emily's mark had been made. The lady with two different shoes was now discussing tires with the man on the couch, and a newcomer to the group was putting on a fresh pot of coffee.

I realized, sadly, that for some reason, we outgrow a child's innocent world and become slave to society's sometimes odd social rules. A child can teach us things about the world, things that we, too, once knew, but quickly forgot ... things we need to be reminded of, again and again.

Because sometimes a child understands what it truly means to be human more than an adult does. And best of all, she isn't afraid to act on her feelings.

This story first appeared in *The Perry County News*, April 21, 1997, and is reprinted with the kind permission of the publisher.

*P*retty much all the honest truth telling in the world is done by children.

—Oliver Wendell Holmes

Stripped of Pride— Children Are the Teachers of Humility

By Joan K. Nuxoll

I often get a glimpse of God through the people in my life. Many times, the person God uses is a child. When I consider the subject of pride, children are a do-it-yourself kit to becoming a monk. There are two ways to be given the grace of humility. One way is to ask God for it; the other way is to become a parent. My children have been embarrassing me for 15 years.

I think God gives the babies a pep talk before they leave heaven. Together they look down at us and God says, "Those two people are going to be your parents. They'll love you for the rest of their lives. You must give them a wonderful gift: strip them of their pride. Now, go down there and get to it."

And children listen to God. My own started their work the very first time we took them out in public: they would vomit down my back. And of course, I never found the mess until I arrived home, so I imagine everyone said, "It was a beautiful baptism, but what was that running down the back of the mother's dress?"

Sometime during their toddler years, each of our children seized an opportunity to bring all the neighborhood kids into the bathroom to look for a Band-Aid—while I was taking a bath. (There are variations on this. Sometimes they show their friends how my nose hairs go in and out while I'm taking a nap. Sometimes, they pile things on the bathroom scales trying to get the numbers to go as high as when Mommy stands on it.) I have learned that all toddlers have perfect memories and a compulsion to tell everything they know to anyone who will listen. My mailman knows more about me than my mother does.

As the children get older, they continue their mission from God, but they become a little more sophisticated: they carefully select their audience. Every child has his own style, but my boys prefer to include school principals, angry neighbor ladies, policemen, and doctors. Favorite subjects are personal hygiene (anyone's), our checkbook balance, skin conditions, our dog's sex life, traffic violations, and (their favorite) the category they fondly refer to as "Mother's most embarrassing moments."

I know this is a universal gift from God because in church today, I finally saw it happen to someone else. They were a nice-looking couple. Their young daughter was not only the picture of childhood innocence, but she was clean, her hair was in ribbons and braids, and she was wearing a pretty little ruffled dress and shiny "church shoes." The little girl made a favorable impression on all of us sitting in the last 10 pews as she quietly followed her parents up the aisle, genuflected deeply and reverently, and took her place between them. Her parents knelt in prayer and became quite oblivious to their sweet little daughter's behavior.

Their precious daughter turned backward in the pew and started making monstrous faces at her former admirers. During the mass, she assumed this backward position when her parents looked elsewhere, and carried on a monologue for us by clearly miming obscene words. (My children commented later that her family probably has cable TV and that she picked up her filthy vocabulary from what she viewed on cable channels.) The parents worshipped in ignorance of their daughter's behavior.

Needless to say, I was distracted. I was unable to hold my attention on the liturgy, so horrified and repulsed was I by this little girl's horrible behavior.

Finally, I simply gave up and let myself focus on the child. I tried to redeem the distraction by turning it into prayer. I thought about how I often make judgments, good and bad, based on appearances, and I asked God to forgive me for that. I thought how oblivious the parents were to their daughter's actions, and that reminded me of how often I am close—very close—to someone who is hurting or in need and remain oblivious to that. I asked God for more sensitivity. Then I thought about how grateful I am that my own children are not at all naughty like that little girl, that my children have been taught much better manners, that my children don't even know most of the words that little girl was obnoxiously mouthing … Hello pharisee!

I think God loves to catch me at that. I think God absolutely delights in it. I imagine God saying "Aha! Gotcha!" with a warm, nonjudgmental smile.

No sooner did my superior thoughts flit across my mind than God sent a living parable into my life: my two older sons started to argue at the end of our pew. The fact that they were arguing was nothing unusual, but the fact that they were doing it in church was absolutely infuriating.

I leaned over and tried to catch the eye of my eldest, who was violently wrestling a songbook out of the hands of his brother. I sternly whispered his name, trying to get his attention more by the tone of my whisper than with volume. He glared at me defiantly and said, "Ah, forget it!" in a loud, belligerent voice. I felt like everyone in that church turned to look.

Later that afternoon, when I had calmed myself and was ready to tackle the problem, I called the two boys from their bedroom. They both apologized for their behavior. The older one explained that his words, "Forget it," were directed at his brother instead of me, and they were meant to be a message of defeat rather than one of defiance toward me. (The jury is still out on that one.)

I am satisfied with the dialogue, discipline, apologies, and forgiveness which came from that conversation. That part of the day, of course, happened without a witness.

I am now left with the reassuring, relentless reminder that we are all one. I am left, as are the parents of the little girl, with nothing more than trust—trust that parents everywhere are mutually understanding, laughing, and supporting one another through this vocation of parenthood. We are all one in the project, and none of us is safe from the gift of humility bestowed by our children. We are all one, even with those couples who as yet have no children; somewhere there is a child waiting to vomit down their backs, too.

> *Teach us delight in simple things, / And mirth that has no bitter springs.*
>
> — Rudyard Kipling, *The Children's Song*

A Child's Perspective
By Rev. Dr. Richard B. Gilbert

The story has been told before. A Sunday School teacher gives children paper and crayons and invites them to draw a religious picture. A youngster pipes up, "I am going to draw a picture of God." The teacher reminds her, "But no one knows what God looks like," to which the child replies, "That's because I haven't finished the picture yet."

The rare gift of children—and it is a gift—is that they keep it all simple. Faith really is simple. It's *life* that gets complicated. We look at life as a series of maladies: paying bills, world crime, health costs, family violence, guns, declining standards in schools. Children check out what's in their school lunch, how much time they have until the bus arrives, and consider who will tuck them in at bedtime.

It isn't that children don't see the other problems; they do. But they see them from their own perspective, a perspective of trust, care, and belief. There is an enthusiastic presence in a child—(at least until the adult world tarnishes it) that says, "I count. I belong. I am special." There is the Gospel, the Incarnate Word, at its best.

To illustrate this, a recent cartoon depicted a priest trying to explain the Trinity. (There's a hopeless challenge for children of all ages.) The priest says, "The Trinity is one," and a little child jumps up to exclaim, "And I am three."

Something happens when we lose the child within us. Growing up has become growing *away from*. I am not talking about the need for our independence, the need for exploring life on our own. The Loving Father even allowed his son, the prodigal, as we call him, to wander off and discover life. We lose many things as adults, but especially the childlike innocence that allows us to believe that we are empowered to draw the definitive picture of God, and that being three really matters.

Faith is still simple. Only adults complicate it with our apparent knowledge. Children are our best teachers, even when it comes to matters of faith. Let them teach you.

"I have a dream, that my four little children will one day live in a nation where they will not be judged by the color of their skin but by the content of their character."

— Martin Luther King, Jr.

God Is Color-blind

By Kathryn Lankston

Although it was not our "geographic parish," we joined Saint Cronin Catholic Church shortly after we moved to the city. Its focus on social justice and inner-city ministries appealed to our sense of living the gospel.

Making last-minute preparations for my group of confirmation candidates one Sunday morning, in the building that served as the parish's religious education facility, I listened to my 11-year-old daughter, Bess, talking with her friend. "Are any of those kids out there in your class, Bess?" her friend asked, as they looked out the second-story window down on the group gathering below. Bess's friend was from our "geographic parish" and had come along with us that morning to go to Mass at Saint Cronin's. "Yeah, that one girl is. See the one in the pink coat and the white hat? The one who's laughing and spinning in circles? She's in my class."

After several seconds of evidently searching the crowd for the girl in the pink coat and the white hat, Bess's friend exclaims, "Oh, I see her! The black girl, right?"

With immediate indignation, Bess quipped, "What does black have to do with it? She's wearing a pink coat and a white hat and she's laughing and spinning in circles!"

Hearing Bess's raised voice and the content of her statement, I was brought to a deep sense of humility. Of course, what does black have to do with it! Why would we use the color of a person's skin as a primary identifying characteristic?

Like God, Bess first saw a *human being* in a pink coat and a white hat laughing and spinning in circles—not a black person. Like God, Bess saw many other distinct and unique characteristics to that young girl's person beyond the color of her skin. Like God, Bess seemed to be color-blind.

If help and salvation are to come, they can only come from the children, for the children are the makers of men.

— Maria Montessori

God and Sinner Reconciled
By Fr. Joe Weigman

I worked for a few years in consumer marketing. One year at our company Christmas party, I remember standing around, talking "company talk" with my co-workers. That particular year, most of our conversations were about profits being down, costs going up, and our biggest competitor gaining ground.

There were also stories going around about one of the vice-presidents who had recently resigned after it became known that he had had several affairs with company employees. "What a creep," I remember hearing. Despite the approaching holiday and the party atmosphere, there was not much joy in the room.

Then, one of the department heads announced to us that her son and his fourth-grade classmates were going to sing Christmas carols for us. Right on cue, the children marched in and stood at the front of the room. They sang a medley of traditional Christmas songs. When the singing ended, we all clapped and told them what a good job they had done. It did not take us long, however, to get back to our "grown-up" company talk.

We didn't notice that one little girl remained at the front of the room while her classmates left. Startling most of us, she began to sing a solo of "Hark, the Herald

Angels Sing." She had a beautiful voice. When she finished, we all clapped again, then returned to our conversations. "He ruined his career," someone else said about the vice-president. "It's a shame, because he was on the fast-track."

While we thought that the little girl with the beautiful voice was finished, she was not. She began the same carol again, and sang with more gusto than before, "Peace on earth and mercy mild, God and sinner reconciled."

She finished, and so we began our discussion again. "I can't believe he would do that to his wife," someone else said about the vice-president. Once again, the little girl began to sing. This time, she repeated over and over the words, "Peace on earth and mercy mild, God and sinner reconciled."

It suddenly dawned on me: those words applied in a special way to those of us in the room who could not stop talking about the sins of the vice-president. Through the little girl with the beautiful voice, God was communicating to us the real significance of the Incarnation. Christmas is about more than Jesus in a manger; it is about God becoming one of us, to assure us of his love and forgiveness.

In the years since that Christmas party, I have often remembered the little girl with the beautiful voice who sang "Hark, the Herald Angels Sing" for us, especially when I am tempted to dwell on the sins of others while ignoring my own. The Church celebrates the Incarnation for about three weeks of the year, but the reality of God's love and forgiveness, of us and of others, is something to remind ourselves of day after day after day.

God at Work Series

- *God at Work…
  in Times of Loss.* #20096

- *God at Work…
  in Times of Trouble.* #20095

- *God at Work…
  Through the Voices of
  Children.* #20097

Available at your favorite bookstore
or gift shop, or directly from:
One Caring Place, Abbey Press,
St. Meinrad, IN 47577
(800) 325-2511
www.onecaringplace.com